Delicious & Easy Weight Loss Recipes for Beginners

Giulia .T Bradshaw

<u>Funny helpful tips:</u>

In a world filled with noise, find solace in the moments of silence that allow you to reconnect with yourself.

Invest in robust IT infrastructure; it supports operations and growth.

Delicious & Easy Weight Loss Recipes for Beginners :
Discover the Ultimate Guide to Healthy Eating with Quick and
Tasty Weight Loss Recipes for a Happier You

<u>Life advices:</u>

Avoid keeping score; mutual love is not a competition.

Set clear financial goals; they provide motivation and a roadmap for success.

Introduction

This book offers a comprehensive collection of delicious and nutritious low-carb recipes designed to aid in weight loss. The guide emphasizes the benefits of meal-prepping, the essential equipment needed, and provides a variety of recipes for breakfast, lunch, dinner, and super-food snacks.

The guide begins by highlighting the advantages of meal-prepping, such as time-saving, portion control, and ensuring healthier eating habits. It lists the helpful equipment required for successful meal-prepping.

For breakfast, the guide presents a range of low-carb options, including Almond Joy Microwave Muffin, Black and Blue Smoothie, Breakfast Casserole, and Butter Pecan Waffles. It also offers creative recipes like Chocolate Muffin and Huevos Rancheros.

The lunch section features a selection of satisfying meals, such as Albacore Tuna Vinaigrette Salad, Chicken Lettuce Wraps, Cobb Salad, and Shrimp and Cucumber Salad. There are also heartier options like Chicken Quesadillas and Chili Mac.

The dinner section offers a variety of flavorful dishes, including Beef Stroganoff with Protein Noodles, Chicken Parmesan over Protein Pasta, and Italian Chicken with Asparagus and Artichoke Hearts. There are also unique recipes like Kabobs with Peanut Curry Sauce and Cajun Blackened Fish with Cauliflower Salad.

For those in need of quick and healthy snacks, the guide provides options like Berry-Choco-Cherry Protein Bars, Chipotle Kale Chips, and Smoked Salmon Dip. Additionally, it offers alternatives like Vietnamese Spring Rolls with Peanut Sauce and Zucchini and Asparagus Fries.

Overall, this book offers a variety of flavorful, low-carb recipes that make meal-prepping easier and support weight loss goals. Whether for breakfast, lunch, dinner, or snacks, the guide's recipes cater to various tastes and dietary preferences, making it an excellent resource for those seeking healthier eating habits and successful weight loss.

Contents

Chapter 1: Why Should I Meal Prep?

Meal prepping is a new concept for busy cooks to help them plan the week with pre-planned meals and quick access to the ingredients.

Everybody has schedule overload these days, especially if you work full-time, kids to take to school, home from school, soccer and theatre practice, after hours work obligations, meals to cook and a house to clean.

Don't you feel overwhelmed and tired already?

The basics of meal-prep works like this.

- You plan the menus for the week for breakfast, lunch, and supper. Add snacks if you wish, we have plenty listed in the last chapter.
- You make the list of ingredients for the week.
- You buy the ingredients and the proper storage containers.
- You cook everything on one afternoon, usually in two hours or less.
- You refrigerate and freeze the contents, labeling each packet.
- When you are ready to eat, you heat them and serve them.

You have just eliminated at least six hours of work a week, and decreased spending, and stayed on your high protein, low carb diet.

Hurray! Victory!

Benefits of Meal-Prepping

At first, meal prepping may seem like a lot of work that takes up a weekend afternoon, very precious time in my household. There are so many exciting benefits of meal-prepping I'm not quite sure where to start. Here are a few for your consideration:

1. Your kitchen time will be cut by as much as 75 percent, once you get the hang of it and make it a personal habit.
2. Your grocery bill will instantly drop. One of the reasons is because you are buying in bulk and all at one time. Another of the reasons is the impulse factor. Have you ever gone to the grocery store for just one item and came home with a trunk load of many unnecessary purchases, all because you were hungry?
3. Using the concepts of meal prep allows you to know what you are eating with the correct portion size. Eating out is too much a temptation to buy the wrong dinner choices, and eating leftovers so you don't have to store them is still overeating.
4. With the extra time you gain from eating properly and preparing your meals once a week, you can now add the exercise plan to your day that you've always wanted to start, but never had enough time.

The Helpful Equipment

Note this equipment is helpful, but not a necessity. Everything can be cooked on a stove, using a skillet, or pots and pans. Knives can be used to cut and plates can function as cutting boards. However, since the point of meal-prep is to save both time and money, these appliances pay for themselves in many ways.

A Crock-pot

This ageless appliance lets you cook and rest at the same time. Although there are only a few crock-pot recipes within these covers, these will not be the only recipes you prepare. If you use a crockpot on cooking day, you can use a larger and less expensive cut of meat. This can be a real savings.

Skillets that are oven proof and non-stick

Most likely if you cook any meals ever you have a skillet or two. In this cookbook, we strive to mess up less dishes. Some of the recipes require browning and then baking. An ovenproof skillet can do both, eliminating one more dish to wash.

At least 3 mixing bowls in large, medium and small sizes

It may be likely that you have these, but not everyone does. As you double or triple recipes when you cook, you will need more than one size and more than one in quantity.

A Blender

Some soups taste better when blended to a creamy puree. It is always easier and tastier to emulsify salad dressings, instead of whipping them by hand in a bowl. You do not have to buy an expensive model as 5 or 6 settings will be enough for the blending instructions we have included.

A Food Processor

When you are preparing multiple meals, using a food processor to chop, slice, and dice saves so much energy and time. The foods are also healthier. Did you know that purchased shredded cheese can include 10 percent wood pulp, commonly called saw dust? When you are purchasing 10 pounds of cheese, you are receiving eight pounds of cheese and two pounds of sawdust. What's more, you are eating it! Save your health by shredding your own blocks of cheese with the food processor. You can freeze it for later use and know the contents of what you are eating.

Good quality sharp knives

Sharp knives make cutting faster and help to keep you from cutting yourself by pressing too hard.

Cutting Boards

Cutting Boards come in several materials and sizes. They protect surfaces and allow the air to circulate underneath while the baked goods cool.

Keep in mind that the construction materials of a cutting board will determine its cleanliness. For example:

Bamboo cutting boards are self-healing. This allows the cuts made by knives to heal on their own. The bamboo cutting boards are very good to knives as they do not dull them quickly. Bamboo is a porous material, which allows bacteria to seep into the cuts. Even disinfecting promptly after use will never eliminate the germs that have accumulated on a wood cutting board.

Plastic boards are non-porous and can be cleaned with stronger chemicals. They still incur cuts and need thorough disinfecting immediately. They will not damage your knives.

Glass cutting boards do not receive cuts, are easy to clean, and can take any kind of chemical disinfectant. They damage knives very quickly and you will be replacing your knives about every three months. Which is less expensive, replacing the cutting boards or the knives?

Glass canning jars with lids, pint sized and quart sized

One of the lesser known secrets is that salad stored in a Ball or Mason jar with a tight sealing lid will stay fresh in the refrigerator for seven full days! This makes the dinner salad, stored in a quart jar, easy to place into serving plates. Salads stored in pint jars are perfect for toting in the thermal lunch bag for a healthy lunch. The salad dressing can be included in the jar and will still be fresh.

Foil containers

These can be expensive, but dollar stores have these priced better than grocery stores. Buy the containers that include lids, baking sizes and the individual sizes.

Plastic containers

Use the food prep containers that are custom designed for Meal-prep. These have no BPAs, are apportioned in the right serving sizes, and are inexpensive. They are dishwasher safe, freezer safe, and can be used in the microwave. Buy enough containers for all your family members to eat three meals a day for one week. You will also need zip-lock freezer bags, pint-sized and snack-sized. Using leftover whipped topping bowls or margarine containers can be less expensive, but they are not constructed to be heated in the microwave or stored for long-term in the freezer.

Getting Started with Meal-Prep

Begin by choosing your menus for each meal.

You can either print your recipes, write them on cards, or whatever convenient method you have for storing them for easy access.

Get a one-week planning calendar. Try to find one that has a menu planner and a shopping list feature. This is so convenient for the shopping part of the process.

Use your computer to create a spreadsheet. Make a list of ingredients in column A. Go through every recipe and list every ingredient with the quantity after it, like this:

- Apples 2
- Garlic salt ½ tsp
- Garlic salt 2 T
- Cheese, cheddar 1 cup, hand-shredded

There is a method for this process. After you have listed every ingredient for the week, then sort by column A alphabetically. Your like items will appear one after the other.

Now add the totals for each item in column B. for example, garlic salt total will be 2 T and ½ tsp. Knowing that 3 tsp equals 1 Tablespoon, we will list the total as

- Garlic salt, 6 ½ tsp.

You now have an alphabetized list of every ingredient you need for the week. If you need to purchase it, you can highlight it on the page. This list is very useful when shopping and while you are in the cooking phase.

Add **Salad extras** to your grocery list. There are days you will want to bulk up the salad choice. Keep these items in your pantry to throw a handful into the jar of salad you will have for dinner.

Examples:

- Chopped radishes
- dried cranberries
- hand-shredded cheeses of every type
- nuts
  - walnuts
  - almonds
  - macadamia nuts
  - pecans
  - peanuts
  - hazelnuts

- artichoke hearts
- jicama
- pickled okra

On Meal Prep Cooking Day

Bring everything out from the pantry and fridge that you need for the meals.
Try to choose like foods in your menus, for example, serve two chicken dishes during the week to save money.

Line up all the containers you will need to store the food. This makes the process go much faster.

Cook the meals and separate into portions. Have something cooking on the stove, something in the stove, and something being blended. Don't forget the crock-pot to cook a pork roast or a large quantity of chicken breasts. Let all dishes cool before you freeze or refrigerate.

Tape or label with a Sharpie on the outside of the container what the meal is, or number the containers.

Place your menu cards for the week in a visible place, like on the refrigerator.

It is helpful to number the meals 1-21, and place the corresponding number temporarily on the menu card. This reference will allow you to quickly determine which condiments, spices, vegetables and meats are for which specific meal. Alternatively, the meals can be labeled with the day they are to be served, and the meal for which they are prepared.

Cooking and preparing 4 lunches a week gives a cooking holiday for day 5. This is a good day to treat yourself to lunch with a friend. When you are cooking the Sunday dinner, if you choose a large cut of meat, the leftover meat can be used in the meal-prep for the following week. This will be one less meat you will need to cook on meal-prep cooking day.

Meal-Prep Ideas to Make Things Simple

If this is your first time to meal prep, start small. This could be the week you just make lunches ahead. Assemble your Mason or Ball jars and prep your salads.

Make breakfast next. Remember, you are expanding the concept one meal at a time. Breakfast can be easy muffins for this week. Two or three batches, both savory and sweet, can fill you up and make a fast commuting breakfast. Add some Greek yogurt and you have more protein and calcium, a double win.

You don't have to do it all on the same day. Cook a crockpot full of fresh veggies and place them in your seven dinner containers. Make a big pot of mashed cauliflower at the same time, and one of low-carb whole wheat pasta. Now you have a week's worth of veggies and starches already completed. Cook a roasted chicken or two in the oven, add a pork tenderloin, and you have cooked dinner for the week! Wasn't that easy to do?

Tomorrow tackle the lunches, and if they are just salads, make two batches of muffins. Add a quiche to the oven. Breakfast and lunch are now done! It probably took less than two hours for either cooking days, and saved you at least five hours of frustration during the work week. As you get more comfortable, you will be able to cook two weeks at a time, only having to make salads on one cooking day and cooking the whole shebang the next weekend.

Instead of cooking the same vegetable for all week, make two pans of roasted vegetables. This way, you are still cooking efficiently but you are also adding variety. The most frustrating thing about meal-prepping is the lack of variety on the menu. This is not because there are limited foods to prepare; it is because we tend to focus on what we know so we cook the same thing often. When you have posted the menu cards on the fridge, like we discussed earlier, then you will automatically eliminate them from your menu choices for the next week. The cards aren't in the stack from which to choose so you will be forced to pick something different. It goes without saying, do not place the cards in the menu selection pile until you have eaten every meal that has been prepared for the week.

Don't forget to boil a dozen eggs every week for meals on the go. Already cooked boiled eggs stored in the fridge will stay fresh for a week after cooking. These are so useful for egg and olive salad, additional protein in your daily salad, and the constant standby meal, a tuna salad.

Bake your "hard-boiled" eggs in the oven. Fill a muffin tin with a dozen eggs, pre-heat the oven to 350F, and bake in the hot oven 34 minutes. Immerse immediately in cold water for 9 minutes if you want to peel them. You can also leave them unpeeled in the refrigerator and place an X on the egg to signify that it is cooked.

You don't have to eat a cooked breakfast every day. Prepare smoothie ingredients with meal prep by placing the appropriate servings in muffin tins and freeze them. After they are frozen, you can either place them in snack bags or leave them in the tin. Two muffins of fruit equal one serving size for a smoothie.

The number one rule for making meal prepping work for you is to have fun!

Have a meal-prep party. Invite two or three friends over and all of you cook at once. You will have new cooking ideas and recipes, the hours will fly by, and you can form an assembly line. This really makes the meals go faster. In addition, you've carved out time for your good friends, shared a lot of laughter and a few mistakes, and turned what could have been tedious into a fun afternoon.

Make your meals for the week based on a theme. Pick a Mexican week, an Italian week, a steak or chicken week, an Asian food week, etc. Cook a mystery dinner once a week to try a new recipe.

Buy the newest containers that are fun to fill.

Freeze in appropriate sized containers. If you want one serving of chili rellenos, but have a huge pan of them, you will revert to your old habits, or eating out.

Be organized and label everything. Either purchase the freezer containers that stack or place everything in zip-lock baggies. If you choose the baggie method, tape the ends of the bags completely sealed with white freezer tape. Write the meal on the bag and then lay them flat to freeze. (A cookie sheet is good for this if you don't have much space.) When the soup or sauce has completely frozen, place in a plastic bin on its side, like a file folder. Now you have an easy way to pull soup or sauce without digging through the baggies.

Keep an ongoing rotation list so the foods don't get stale. Pinterest is a good place to simply record what you have, what you tried, and what you hate. Use a fourth column to list what you want to do next week. If you list the meals on the cooking day, then you will know the variety in the freezer. Things will come up to change your food plans.

I hope that you have found enough hints and benefits to make meal-prepping a fun and interesting endeavor for your cooking day.

This book is chock-full of recipes that will get you started and on the road to successful and quick meal preparation. Good luck and have fun!

Chapter 2: Breakfast

Almond Joy Microwave Muffin

Prep time: 3 min; **Cook time:** 1 min
Serving Size: 1; **Serves:** 1; **Calories:** 207
Total Fat: 16.8g; **Protein:** 9.7g; **Total Carbs:** 3.7g
Dietary Fiber: 3; **Sugar:** 0; **Sodium:** 300mg

Ingredients

- 2 T almond flour
- 1 tsp Coconut Flour
- 1 packet Splenda
- 1/4 tsp Baking Powder
- Sprinkle of Salt
- 1 Egg
- 1 T butter
- 1 tsp cocoa

Directions

1. Combine the dry ingredients into a microwaveable mug.
2. Quickly whip the egg and the oil together.
3. Stir into the dry mixture.
4. Microwave on high for 1 minute.
5. Toast with butter.

Prep Instructions

Place all dry ingredients in zip-lock baggies, 1 recipe per bag. Do not premix the eggs and oil. Wait until morning for combining.

Black and Blue Smoothie

Prep time: 4 min; **Cook time:** 0 min
Serving Size: 1; **Serves:** 1; **Calories:** 221
Total Fat: 9.8g; **Protein:** 21.8g; **Total Carbs:** 10g
Dietary Fiber: 5.8g; **Sugar:** 1g; **Sodium:** 0mg

Ingredients

- ¼ cup Frozen Blueberries
- ¼ cup Frozen Blackberries
- 1 C unsweetened soy or almond milk
- 1 tsp vanilla
- 1 scoop (your choice) vanilla whey protein powder
- 2 packets sweetener of your choice
- 3 tsp flaxseeds

Directions

1. Mix the ingredients and emulsify by blending.
2. Pulse four times or until desired thickness.
3. Pour into a glass and enjoy.

Prep Instructions

Combine berries in freezer bags and place in the freezer. Combine sweetener of your choice, flaxseeds, and protein powder in zip-lock bags. Combine milk and vanilla in 1 cup containers in the fridge.

Breakfast Casserole

Prep time: 4 min; **Cook time:** 19 min
Serving Size: 1 dish; **Serves:** 4; **Calories:** 195
Total Fat: 11g; **Protein:** 19g; **Total Carbs:** 3g
Dietary Fiber: 1g; **Sugar:** 0; **Sodium:** 112mg

Ingredients

- 8 oz Sausage, Cooked and Crumbled
- 1 cup hot salsa
- 4 eggs
- 2 chopped green onions
- ¼ cup hand-shredded pepper jack or cheddar cheese
- ½ bell pepper, chopped, your choice of color

Directions

1. Place oven rack to the middle shelf setting.
2. Heat oven to 400 degrees.
3. Cook the peppers until soft.
4. Spray or grease the baking dishes excessively. Eggs stick when baked.
5. Layer ingredients in 4 individual baking dishes, like Corning ware "grab-its", any bakeware that holds one cup servings.
6. Layer with sausage first, then peppers, then cheese.
7. Add one whipped egg to each baking dish. Sprinkle with green onions.
8. Bake for 18 minutes, until eggs are set.

Freezing Instructions

Place cooled casseroles in individual freezer bags. Reheat in microwave for 2-3 minutes until hot.

Breakfast Mexican Omelet

Prep time: 4 min; **Cook time:** 9 min
Serving Size: 1; Serves: 1; Calories: 275
Total Fat: 21; **Protein:** 17g; **Total Carbs:** 3.2g
Dietary Fiber: 2g; **Sugar:** 2g; **Sodium:** 230mg

Ingredients

- ½ T lime juice
- 2 eggs
- 1 tsp water
- 1 T crumbled bacon
- 1/2 T butter
- ¼ avocado
- ½ c hand-shredded Mexican cheese
- 2 T Pace Thick and Chunky Medium Salsa

Directions

1. Melt the butter in a microwaveable bowl in the microwave.
2. Quickly whip the wet ingredients in a microwaveable bowl, can be the same bowl as before.
3. Microwave for one minute.
4. Place on warm plate.
5. Top with all the rest of the ingredients.

Prep Instructions

Combine the wet ingredients in a zip-lock bag, except the butter and water. Refrigerate. Combine the water and butter in a zip-lock bag.

Butter Pecan Waffles

Prep time: 9 min; **Cook time:** 4 min
Serving Size: 1; **Serves:** 8; **Calories:** 181
Total Fat: 13g; **Protein:** 9g; **Total Carbs:** 5g
Dietary Fiber: 2g; **Sugar:** 3g; **Sodium:** 178mg

Ingredients

- 1 cup soy flour
- 2 packets Splenda
- 3 tsp baking powder
- ¾ cup buttermilk
- 1 T butter
- ½ tsp baking soda
- 3 eggs
- 2 T vanilla
- ½ cup water
- 2 T sugar free butter rum flavoring
- ½ c pecans

Directions

1. Combine everything except the pecans.
2. Use ¼ c batter for cooking the waffle.
3. Cook until crisp.
4. Top with pecans and sugar free syrup.

Freezing Instructions

After the waffle is cool, place 1 per zip-lock bag. Warm by toasting in the toaster.

Cheese Blintz with Blueberries

Prep time: 9 min; **Cook time:** 4 min
Serving Size: 1; **Serves:** 1; **Calories:** 427
Total Fat: 23g; **Protein:** 39g; **Total Carbs:** 14g
Dietary Fiber: 3g; **Sugar:** 10g; **Sodium:** 330mg

Ingredients

- 1 medium egg
- 1 T half & half
- 1 scoop protein shake powder, vanilla
- 1 pat of butter
- 1 tsp of olive oil
- 2 T ricotta cheese
- 1 T Greek yogurt, plain
- 1 packet sweetener
- 1 tsp cinnamon
- ½ c blueberries

Directions

1. Combine the ricotta cheese, Greek yogurt, sweetener and cinnamon in a bowl, mix well.
2. Combine the egg, protein powder, and cream. Whisk until all lumps are dissolved and mixture is well-blended.
3. Coat a non-stick skillet with the olive oil.
4. At medium heat, melt butter in the skillet and pour the batter on top.
5. Swirl the skillet until the batter is evenly distributed.
6. When the batter has set, gently turn the blintz to the other side.
7. Let cook for one minute until the batter is set, but not browned.

8. Gently fold half the blueberries into the filling.
9. Place the filling in the middle of the blintz.
10. Roll into a pancake and serve with the remaining blueberries.

Prep Instructions
Mix the filling and place in the fridge in a covered container. Place the blueberries in a zip-lock bag and place in the freezer.

Chocolate Muffin

Prep time: 4 min; **Cook time:** 1 min
Serving Size: 1; **Serves:** 1; **Calories:** 207
Total Fat: 24g; **Protein:** 10g; **Total Carbs:** 16g
Dietary Fiber: 11g; **Sugar:** 0; **Sodium:** 308mg

Ingredients

- 1 T plain flour
- 1 scoop of Chocolate Protein Powder
- ½ tsp baking powder
- 1 T of cocoa powder
- 2 packets Splenda
- 1 T butter
- 1 egg

Directions

1. Mix the dry ingredients in a cup
2. Combine the wet ingredients
3. Add the wet ingredients into the cup of dry
4. Microwave for one minute

Freezing Instructions

Place individual muffins in a zip-lock bag and place in the freezer.
Microwave one minute to thaw and serve.

Cinnamon Chocolate Smoothie

Prep time: 4 min; **Cook time:** 0 min
Serving Size: 1; **Serves:** 1; **Calories:** 273
Total Fat: 15g; **Protein:** 33g; **Total Carbs:** 9g
Dietary Fiber: 20g; **Sugar:** 2g; **Sodium:** 214mg

Ingredients

- ½ c firm Tofu
- 2 T cocoa powder
- 1 scoop chocolate protein powder
- 2 T cinnamon
- 2 sweetener packets
- 1 c almond milk, unsweetened
- 4 ice cubes

Directions

1. Place all the ingredients in a blender, pulse until desired consistency, and serve.

Prep Instructions
Refrigerate the tofu. Place all the dry ingredients into one snack sized zip-lock bag.

Denver Omelet

Prep time: 4 min; **Cook time:** 1 min;
Serving Size: 1; **Serves:** 1; **Calories:** 605
Total Fat: 46g; **Protein:** 39g; **Total Carbs:** 6g
Dietary Fiber: 2g; **Sugar:** 0g; **Sodium:** 380mg

Ingredients

- 2 T butter
- ¼ cup chopped onions
- ¼ cup green bell pepper, diced
- ¼ cup halved grape tomatoes
- 2 eggs
- ¼ cup chopped ham

Directions

1. Sautee the onions and bell pepper, with the butter, in a small skillet.
2. Whip the eggs and mix the ingredients in a bowl.
3. Microwave for one minute.

Prep Instructions

Pre-cook the peppers and onions and place in zip-lock freezer bags by portions, add the ham to the bags. Freeze. The night before making, place the peppers mix in the fridge to thaw, or microwave for one minute before adding to the whipped egg to make.

Ham Rollups

Prep time: 9 min; **Cook time:** 0 min
Serving Size: 1; **Serves:** 6; **Calories:** 228
Total Fat: 18g; **Protein:** 18g; **Total Carbs:** 6g
Dietary Fiber: 7g; **Sugar:** 0g; **Sodium:** 358mg

Ingredients

- 6 Tortilla Factory low carb whole wheat tortillas
- 8 oz. whipped cream cheese
- 6 slices ham, the rectangular kind, cut in half
- ½ cup pickle dill relish
- 2 T mayonnaise
- 2 T Dijon mustard

Directions

1. Combine cream cheese, dill relish, mustard and mayo in a bowl.
2. Lay one tortilla out on waxed paper or saran wrap.
3. Place one slice of ham on top.
4. Spread ham slices with the cream cheese mixture.
5. Roll the entire piece up.
6. Cut in half.
7. Refrigerate until serving, 1 whole tortilla is one serving, so if cut in half, is still one serving.

Prep Instructions

Place serving size per individual zip-lock bag.

Huevos Rancheros

Prep time: 9 min; **Cook time:** 19 min
Serving Size: ¼; **Serves:** 4; **Calories:** 277;
Total Fat: 17g; **Protein:** 20g; **Total Carbs:** 8g;
Dietary Fiber: 13g; **Sugar:** 3g; **Sodium:** 720mg;

Ingredients

- 4 oz. cooked ground sirloin
- ½ cup Pace Salsa Verde
- 4 eggs
- 4 slices Canadian bacon
- 4 Tortilla Factory Low Carb Whole Wheat tortillas
- 4 tsp water
- 4 T butter

Directions

1. Melt the butter in a glass bowl.
2. Quickly whip the egg and water with the butter.
3. Microwave 1 minute.
4. Place the tortilla in the microwave for 10 seconds.
5. Layer as follows: Tortilla, Canadian bacon, ground beef, egg, salsa.

Prep Instructions

Place Canadian bacon, cooked sirloin, and salsa into a zip-lock bag. Freeze or refrigerate. Place the tortillas in the fridge to keep them fresh. Add the eggs, etc. when microwaving

Junior Mint Shake

Prep time: 4 min; **Cook time:** 0
Serving Size: 1; **Serves:** 1; **Calories:** 200
Total Fat: 2g; **Protein:** 39g; **Total Carbs:** 7g
Dietary Fiber: 1g; **Sugar:** 3g; **Sodium:** 348mg

Ingredients

- 2 T cocoa
- 6 oz. COLD water
- ¼ cup protein powder, chocolate
- 3 drops peppermint flavoring
- ½ cup cottage cheese
- 2 packets sweetener

- 5 ice cubes

Directions

1. Mix the ingredients and emulsify by blending.
2. Blend until thick.

Prep Instructions

Combine dry ingredients and place in zip-lock bag. Combine cottage cheese and sweetener and refrigerate.

Sausage Egg Muffins

Prep time: 10min; **Cook time:** 29 min
Serving Size: 1; **Serves:** 12; **Calories:** 200
Total Fat: 39g; **Protein:** 16g; **Total Carbs:** 2g
Dietary Fiber: 0g; **Sugar:** 0; **Sodium:** 370mg

Ingredients

- 12 oz. cooked sausage crumbles
- 12 eggs
- ¼ cup milk
- 2 cups cheddar cheese, sharp, hand-shredded
- ¼ tsp black pepper, or chili pepper

Directions

1. Mix all the ingredients.
2. Pour into 12 greased muffin papers (in a pan).
3. Bake at 375 degrees for 29 minutes.
4. Cool for 4 minutes before serving.

Freezing Instructions

After cooling, place in zip-lock freezer bag. For the best flavor, heat in microwave or toaster oven before eating.

Spicy Deviled Eggs

Prep time: 9 min; **Cook time:** 11 min
Serving Size: 2 eggs; **Serves:** 2; **Calories:** 202
Total Fat: 15g; **Protein:** 12g; **Total Carbs:** 3g
Dietary Fiber: 0g; **Sugar:** 2g; **Sodium:** 20mg

Ingredients

- 4 hard-boiled eggs
- 2 T mayonnaise
- 1 T spicy brown mustard
- 1 T diced green chilies

Directions

1. Boil the eggs for 9 minutes.
2. Slice the eggs in half.
3. Scoop out the yolks.
4. Mix the yolks, the mayo, the mustard and the chilies.
5. Place back in the center of the egg whites.

Prep Instructions
Boil the eggs in advance and place in the fridge.

Spinach and Swiss Quiche

Prep time: 19 min; **Cook time:** 29 min
Serving Size:1/4; **Serves:** 4; **Calories:** 417
Total Fat: 37g; **Protein:** 15g; **Total Carbs:** 4g
Dietary Fiber: 1.5g; **Sugar:** 0g; **Sodium:** 209mg

Ingredients

- 2 tsp butter
- 6 oz. frozen chopped spinach, drained and thawed
- 1 cup cream
- 1 cup hand-shredded swiss cheese, hand-shredded cheese
- ¼ tsp salt
- 1 diced white onion
- 4 eggs
- ⅛ tsp nutmeg
- ¼ tsp black pepper, ground

Directions

1. Heat the oven to 350 degrees.
2. Then spray a pie pan with your choice of cooking spray. Spray liberally as eggs may stick.
3. Cook onions in butter till glassy, then add the spinach and simmer until the water is gone.
4. Mix all of the ingredients in a bowl, including the spices.
5. Pour into the pie pan.
6. Bake for 29 minutes.
7. Cool for 9 minutes and cut into quarters.

Freezing Instructions

Wrap a cooled slice of quiche in saran wrap, then place in a zip-lock bag. Microwave for 1 minute, in two 30-second bursts.

Chapter 3: Lunch

Albacore Tuna Vinaigrette Salad

Prep time: 10 min; **Cook time:** 7 min
Serving Size: 1/4; **Serves:** 4; **Calories:** 231
Total Fat: 20g; **Protein:** 9g; **Total Carbs:** 5.5g
Dietary Fiber: 5g; **Sugar:** 0g; **Sodium:** 265mg

Ingredients

- 1 can albacore tuna, drained
- 1 pound of fresh or frozen asparagus
- ¼ cup walnuts, chopped
- 4 cups baby salad mix
- ½ tsp salt
- ¼ tsp pepper
- 3 tsp finely chopped onion
- 1 tsp spicy brown mustard
- 2 tsp wine vinegar, white or red
- ¼ cup olive oil or garlic sesame oil
- 1 Splenda packet

Directions

1. Mix together the spices and the tuna, set aside.
2. Steam the asparagus for 5-7 minutes until desired crispness.
3. Place the salad mixture onto 4 plates.
4. Divide the asparagus by 4 and place on salad greens.
5. Divide the seasoned tuna by 4 and scatter onto the asparagus and salad.

6.   Sprinkle each salad with the walnuts and serve.

Prep Instructions

Place the tuna mixture in a zip-lock bag and place in the fridge.
Steam the asparagus and place in a zip-lock bag in the fridge. Place
the salad mix in zip-locks in the fridge. Put the walnuts in a bag in
the fridge.

Barbecue Chicken Pizza

Prep time: 19 min; **Cook time:** 29 min
Serving Size: 1 pizza; **Serves:** 8 **Calories:** 285
Total Fat: 12g; **Protein:** 27g **Total Carbs:** 7g
Dietary Fiber: 5g; **Sugar:** 0g; **Sodium:** 100mg

Ingredients

- 1/2 cup G Hughes Smokehouse BBQ Sauce, sugar free
- ½ tsp salt
- 2 cups baking mix, low-carb
- 1 cup water
- 1 chopped red onion
- 1 cup cooked chicken, diced
- ½ cup chopped bell peppers, red, green, yellow assortment
- ½ cup sliced black olives
- 3 T olive oil
- 1 cup mozzarella cheese, hand-shredded
- ½ c parmesan cheese, hand-shredded
- 1 packet Splenda or sweetener of your choice

Directions

1. Set oven to 425 F.
2. Mix into a dough the baking powder, baking mix, Splenda, salt, water and oil.
3. Place on waxed paper and lightly oil. Roll into your pizza crust.
4. Bake for 9 minutes.
5. Remove from heat source and spread the barbecue sauce onto the crust.
6. Layer the toppings, placing the cheeses on top.

7. Bake 15 more minutes until thoroughly warmed and the cheese is melted.
8. Slice into 8 pieces and serve.

Freezing Directions
Place individual slices in a zip-lock freezer bag. Freeze. To serve, heat in microwave one minute.

Bok-Choy Ginger Soup

Prep time: 9 min; **Cook time:** 9 min;
Serving Size: 1 cup; **Serves:** 4; **Calories:** 65
Total Fat: 2g; **Protein:** 7g; **Total Carbs:** 5g
Dietary Fiber: 2g; **Sugar:** 0g; **Sodium:** 100mg

Ingredients

- 3 cups diced green onions
- 2 cups chopped or sliced mushrooms
- 3 tsp fresh grated ginger
- 3 tsp minced garlic
- 4 T tamari
- 2 cups chopped bok-choy
- 1 T cilantro, chopped
- 6 oz. firm tofu, cut into bite sized squares
- 3 T grated carrot
- 1 can diced tomatoes and peppers
- 6 cups chicken broth

Directions

1. Place everything but the green onions, tofu and carrot into a sauce and bring to a boil.
2. Reduce the heat to low-med and cook this for 6 minutes.
3. Stir in the green onions, tofu, and carrots. Cook for 2 more minutes.
4. Serve sprinkled with the cilantro.

Freezing Instructions
Let soup cool thoroughly. Pour into four containers that have lids. Freeze. Microwave 2-3 minutes to serve.

Chicken Lettuce Wraps

Prep time: 10min; **Cook time:** 10min
Serving Size: 1; **Serves:** 1; **Calories:** 145
Total Fat: 1g; **Protein:** 35g; **Total Carbs:** 4g
Dietary Fiber: 1g; **Sugar:** 0g; **Sodium:** 100mg

Ingredients

- 1 chicken breast, boneless, diced into 1-inch size pieces
- 1 cup diced or sliced fresh mushrooms
- ½ cup diced water chestnuts (from a can, drained)
- 1 T olive oil
- 1 T onion, minced
- 1 T minced garlic
- 1 T teriyaki sauce
- garlic powder, only a dash
- onion powder, just a dash
- oregano, one dash
- cayenne pepper, a small dash
- salt /pepper

Directions

1. Mix the ingredients and cook in a skillet until the chicken is done, about 10 minutes.
2. Shred the chicken
3. Place in leaves and roll

Freezing Instructions
Place all ingredients into one freezer bag except the lettuce.
Microwave one minute and serve.

Chicken Quesadillas

Prep time: 4 min; **Cook time:** 4 min
Serving Size: 1; **Serves:** 4; **Calories:** 425g
Total Fat: 25g; **Protein:** 44g; **Total Carbs:** 10g
Dietary Fiber: 9g; **Sugar:** 2g; **Sodium:** 186mg

Ingredients

- 1 cup pepper jack cheese, hand-shredded
- 8 tortillas Tortilla Factory Low Carb Whole Wheat Tortillas
- 8 oz. cooked and shredded Chicken Breast
- 1 chopped and Roasted Bell Pepper
- 2 T Cilantro
- 2 T Butter
- 1 cup plain Greek yogurt

Directions

1. Place ½ pat of butter in a skillet
2. Mix all the ingredients in a bowl except the yogurt
3. Place meat ingredients inside tortillas
4. Toast each side
5. Cut into 4 wedges
6. Top with yogurt and salsa, if desired

Freezing Instructions
Freeze in zip-lock bags. Place the yogurt in the fridge. Heat one
minute in microwave to thaw.

Chili Mac

Prep time: 9 min; **Cook time:** 9 min
Serving Size: 1/4; **Serves:** 4; **Calories:** 480
Total Fat: 24g; **Protein:** 36g; **Total Carbs:** 25g
Dietary Fiber: 6g; **Sugar:** 4g; **Sodium:** 995mg

Ingredients

- 1 lb ground Sirloin
- 1 chopped Onion
- 1 Chili Seasoning Mix, packet
- 1 cup tomato sauce
- 1 small can of Chunky Diced Tomatoes & Green Chilies
- 1 cup hand-shredded sharp cheddar
- 1 packet Splenda
- ½ cup Barilla Proteinplus Elbow macaroni

Directions

1. Boil Barilla Proteinplus Elbow macaroni until done, drain.
2. Brown the sirloin and onions in a large skillet.
3. Add the pasta, tomato sauce, diced tomatoes and green chilies, and chili seasoning mix.
4. Taste to see if you need to add water.
5. Serve in 4 bowls, topping each bowl with the cheddar cheese.

Freezer Directions
Place in four containers with lids, freeze. Microwave 2 minutes to thaw.

Cobb Salad

Prep time: 9 min; **Cook time:** 9 min
Serving Size: 1; **Serves:** 1; **Calories:** 561
Total Fat: 34g; **Protein:** 51g; **Total Carbs:** 3.9g
Dietary Fiber: 6g; **Sugar:** 1g; **Sodium:** 802mg

Ingredients

- 1 slice Bacon or 1 T real bacon bits
- 1 grilled Chicken Breast, which has been cut into thin strips
- 1 cup Spring Mix Salad
- 1/2 cup grape tomatoes, sliced in half
- ½ avocado, sliced into small moons
- ¼ c pepper jack cheese, hand-shredded
- 2 T Ken's Buttermilk Ranch Dressing

Directions

1. Assemble ingredients by sections.
2. Cover the entire bottom of the plate with lettuce.
3. In one corner (relative if you have a round plate) place the tomatoes.
4. In the opposite section place the avocado strips in a fan shape.
5. In the third section place the bacon bits.
6. In the fourth section place the hand-shredded cheese.
7. In the center place the chicken.
8. Drizzle with the salad dressing and serve.

Freezing Instructions

The chicken can be frozen in a zip-lock bag. Microwave 1 minute to serve. The salad can be combined in one bowl, or packed in individual containers and placed in the fridge.

Cream of Mushroom Soup

Prep time: 6 min; **Cook time:** 4 min
Serving Size: 1 cup; **Serves:** 4; **Calories:** 210
Total Fat: 17g; **Protein:** 10g; **Total Carbs:** 3g
Dietary Fiber: 0.5g; **Sugar:** 0g; **Sodium:** 370mg

Ingredients

- 1 pound mushrooms, sliced
- 1 T butter
- ¼ cup cream
- 1 cup water
- ¼ grated Parmesan cheese
- dash of basil
- dash of black pepper

Directions

1. Microwave the mushrooms in the water for 4 minutes. Taste for desired doneness.
2. Drain the mushrooms.
3. Place in blender with butter and cream and Parmesan.
4. Blend until creamy.
5. Pour into bowl and serve

Freezing Instructions

Freeze cooked soup in one cup containers. Microwave one minute, stir, and microwave one more minute to serve.

Cucumber Soup

Prep time: 14 min; **Cook time:** none
Serving Size: 1 cup; **Serves:** 4; **Calories:** 169
Total Fat: 12g; **Protein:** 4g; **Total Carbs:** 9g
Dietary Fiber: 5g; **Sugar:** 6g; **Sodium:** 494mg

Ingredients

- 2 T minced garlic
- 4 c English cucumbers, peeled and diced
- ½ c onion, diced
- 1 T lemon juice
- 1 ½ cups chicken broth
- ½ tsp salt
- 1 diced avocado
- ¼ tsp red pepper flakes
- ¼ cup diced parsley
- ½ cup Greek yogurt, plain

Directions

1. Place all the ingredients and emulsify by blending, except ½ c chopped cucumber.
2. Blend until smooth.
3. Pour into 4 servings.
4. Top with reserved cucumber.

Freezing Instructions
Freeze in one cup containers with lids. Let thaw to serve or microwave 2 minutes to serve hot.

Feta Cucumber Salad

Prep time: 14 min; **Cook time:** none
Serving Size: 1; **Serves:** 4; **Calories:** 142
Total Fat: 10g; **Protein:** 4g; **Total Carbs:** 7g
Dietary Fiber: 3g; **Sugar:** 0g; **Sodium:** 144mg

Ingredients

- 1 head of leaf lettuce, coarsely chopped
- 1 c baby spinach, trimmed, coarsely chopped
- ½ c diced red onion
- 1 c grape tomatoes, sliced in half
- ¼ c Feta cheese, crumbled
- 2 cups plain greek yogurt
- 2 T garlic powder
- 1 T dill
- 2 T lemon juice
- 2 English cucumbers, chopped with peels on
- 2 T olive oil
- ¼ tsp black pepper
- 1 small can black olives, sliced and drained (2.25 oz. can)
- ½ tsp mint or 3 mint leaves

Directions

1. Combine Greek yogurt, dill, garlic powder, mint, lemon juice, olive oil, ½ cup diced cucumber, and black pepper and emulsify by blending.
2. Taste and add salt. Add water by tablespoons if too thick.
3. Arrange on 4 plates the lettuce and spinach, tomatoes, cucumbers, and black olives.
4. Pour the dressing over the salad.
5. Top with the feta cheese.

Prep Directions

Mix the salad dressing and place in fridge in closed containers. Mix the salad and bag or place in covered containers in the fridge. Place the feta cheese in a zip-lock bag in the fridge.

Seven Layer Salad

Prep time: 14 min; **Cook time:** 9 min
Serving Size: 1; **Serves:** 10; **Calories:** 136
Total Fat: 7g; **Protein:** 2g; **Total Carbs:** 9g
Dietary Fiber: 2g; **Sugar:** 0g; **Sodium:** 324mg

Ingredients

- 4 cups shredded butter lettuce
- 4 cups shredded romaine lettuce
- 1 cup peas
- 1 cup diced bell peppers, red and yellow
- 1 cup grape tomatoes, halved
- 1 cup sliced celery
- ½ cup red onion
- ¾ cup Greek yogurt
- ¾ cup mayonnaise
- 3 hard-boiled eggs
- 2 teaspoons cider vinegar
- 1 packet Splenda
- ¼ teaspoon garlic salt
- ½ cup pepper-jack cheese, hand-shredded
- 3 strips cooked bacon, crumbled

Directions

1. Using a large glass pan, 9x13 sized, layer the two lettuces.
2. Layer the peas, then the peppers, then the tomatoes, celery and onion.
3. Place the diced eggs next.
4. Combine the dressing ingredients: yogurt, mayonnaise, vinegar, garlic salt, Splenda, and a dash of black pepper.

5. Spread the dressing over the salad.
6. Garnish with the pepper-jack cheese and bacon.

Storage Instructions
Place in one cup containers. Close with a lid and refrigerate.

Shrimp and Cucumber Salad

Prep time: 4 min; **Cook time:** 0 min
Serving Size: 1/4; **Serves:** 4; **Calories:** 26g
Total Fat: 0g; **Protein:** 2g; **Total Carbs:** 3g
Dietary Fiber: 2g; **Sugar:** 2g; **Sodium:** 157mg

Ingredients

- 2 English cucumbers
- 1/4 cup of red wine vinegar
- 2 tsp of Splenda
- 1/4 tsp salt
- ½ cup cooked shrimp

Directions

1. Peel the cucumbers so that they have stripes down the side.
2. Slice the cucumbers as thin as you can.
3. Mix the dressing of sugar, salt, and vinegar very well
4. Place the cucumbers on a plate
5. Place the shrimp on top
6. Add the dressing and serve.

Prep Directions

Create the entire salad and place in a covered container in the fridge. Will keep 2 days.

Spinach Stuffed Portobello Mushrooms

Prep time: 19 min; **Cook time:** 28 min
Serving Size: 1; **Serves:** 4; **Calories:** 373
Total Fat: 28g; **Protein:** 23g; **Total Carbs:** 7g
Dietary Fiber: 1g; **Sugar:** 2g; **Sodium:** 681mg

Ingredients

- 4 Portobello mushroom tops
- salt /pepper amount to taste
- 1 cup of ricotta cheese
- 1 cup chopped baby spinach
- ½ cup Parmesan cheese, hand-shredded
- 1 small can chopped or sliced black olives (2.25 oz.)
- ½ cup chunky vegetable marinara sauce
- ¼ cup mozzarella cheese, finely hand-shredded

Directions

1. Set the oven to 450F.
2. Line a 9 x 13 inch baking pan with some parchment paper.
3. Place the mushrooms smooth side against the parchment paper.
4. salt /pepper
5. Cook for about 24 minutes. Then remove it from heat source and pour off the liquid.
6. Mix the remaining ingredients except for the mozzarella cheese. Stuff into the tops of the mushrooms.
7. Bake 9 min.
8. Remove from heat source and sprinkle the top with the hand-shredded mozzarella.
9. Broil until the cheese is golden and melted. Serve.

Freezing Instructions

Freeze in individual zip-lock bags. Microwave for 2 minutes to serve.

Tuna Croquettes

Prep time: 4 min; **Cook time: 9 min**
Serving Size: 1 patty; **Serves:** 4; **Calories:** 105g
Total Fat: 5g; **Protein:** 14g; **Total Carbs:** 2g
Dietary Fiber: 1g; **Sugar:** 0; **Sodium:** 265mg

Ingredients

- 1 can tuna, drained
- 1 large egg
- 8 T grated Parmesan cheese
- 2 T flax meal
- dash salt
- dash pepper
- 1 T minced onion

Directions

1. Blend all ingredients except the flax meal
2. Form into patties (¼ cup ea.)
3. Dip both sides in the flax meal
4. Fry until browned on both sides

Freezing Instructions
Place patties in one zip-lock bag each. Microwave 1 minute to serve.

Turkey Wraps

Prep time: 1 min; **Cook time:** none
Serving Size: 1; **Serves:** 1; **Calories:** 154
Total Fat: 9g; **Protein:** 12g; **Total Carbs:** 2g
Dietary Fiber: 0g; **Sugar:** 0g; **Sodium:** 250mg

Ingredients

- 2 slices deli turkey
- 1 oz. provolone cheese, sliced
- 1 lettuce leaf
- 1 tsp spicy brown mustard

Directions

1. Place turkey on the lettuce leaf
2. Spread with brown mustard
3. Top with the Provolone cheese
4. Roll into a burrito shape
5. Eat and enjoy!

Prep Instructions

Roll and prepare the wraps. Place on a paper towel. Place inside a zip-lock bag. Refrigerate until served.

Chapter 4: Dinner

Beef Stroganoff with Protein Noodles

Prep time: 14 min; **Cook time:** 29 min
Serving Size: 1; **Serves:** 1; **Calories:** 559
Total Fat: 23g; **Protein:** 55g; **Total Carbs:** 4g
Dietary Fiber: 13g; **Sugar:** 2g; **Sodium:** 957mg

Ingredients

- 2 oz. Barilla Protein Farfalle Pasta
- ½ cup fresh sliced mushrooms
- 2 Tbls of chopped onion
- 1 T butter
- dash of black pepper
- 6 oz. steak, sliced thinly
- 1 T tomato paste
- ¼ tsp of Dijon mustard
- ½ cup beef broth
- ½ small container plain Greek yogurt

Directions

1. Cook the pasta in water.
2. Place the butter in a Teflon skillet.
3. Next add in the onions, and mushrooms, cook until onions are shiny and water is gone.
4. Add the beef and brown well.
5. Stir in remaining ingredients except the pasta and yogurt.
6. Cook this until the beef is done, approximately 9 minutes.
7. Drain the pasta.

8. If the sauce is too thin, add 1 tsp low carb flax meal and boil to thicken.
9. Turn back down to low. Then add the yogurt to the sauce.
10. Serve the stroganoff over the pasta.

Freezing Instructions
Place dish in appropriate container with a lid and freeze. Heat 2 minutes in a microwave to serve.

Beefy Tostadas

Prep time: 4 min; **Cook time:** 9 min
Serving Size: 2 tostadas; **Serves:** 1; **Calories:** 735
Total Fat: 48g; **Protein:** 66g; **Total Carbs:** 18g
Dietary Fiber: 8g; **Sugar:** 0g; **Sodium:** 708mg

Ingredients

- ¼ pound ground sirloin
- ¼ cup onions, minced
- 1 tsp garlic, minced
- 1 T olive oil
- ½ cup chopped green, red, and yellow peppers
- ½ cup cheddar cheese, mild or sharp, hand-shredded
- 2 Tortilla factory low-carb tortillas
- 2 T butter
- 1 c Greek yogurt, plain
- 2 T salsa verde

Directions

1. Brown the tortillas in the butter. Place on a warm plate.
2. Cook the sirloin, onions, garlic, peppers in the olive oil.
3. Place on the tortillas.
4. Top with the cheese.
5. Add the Greek yogurt.
6. Drizzle with the salsa.

Freezing Directions

Freeze the serving of the meat mixture in a zip-lock bag. Microwave on a plate for one minute to serve. Place the cheese in a zip-lock bag. Add the salsa and the yogurt if you desire. Place the tortillas between wet paper towels and microwave the refrigerated tortillas for 15 seconds before serving.

Bratwurst German Dinner

Prep time: 4 min; **Cook time:** 19 min
Serving Size: 1; **Serves:** 1; **Calories:** 332
Total Fat: 26g; **Protein:** 15g; **Total Carbs:** 8g
Dietary Fiber: 9g; **Sugar:** 4g; **Sodium:** 1188mg

Ingredients

- 1 Bratwurst sausage
- ½ cup sliced onion
- ½ cup sauerkraut, this includes the liquid
- 1 tsp olive oil
- Sprinkle of black pepper

Directions

1. Cook the bratwurst and the onion in the olive oil, in a coated skillet.
2. Remove the bratwurst to a plate.
3. Place the sauerkraut into the skillet and cook 3 min.
4. Add the bratwurst and onion back to warm and mingle the flavors.
5. Sprinkle with black pepper and serve.

Freezing Directions

Place entire serving in one freezer zip-lock bag. Reheat in microwave for 2 minutes.

Cajun Blackened Fish with Cauliflower Salad

Prep time: 9 min; **Cook time:** 9 min
Serving Size: 1; **Serves:** 1; **Calories:** 530
Total Fat: 33.5g; **Protein:** 32g; **Total Carbs:** 5.5g
Dietary Fiber: 4g; **Sugar:** 3g; **Sodium:** 80mg

Ingredients

- 1 cup chopped cauliflower
- 1 tsp red pepper flakes
- 1 T Italian seasonings
- 1 T garlic, minced
- 6 oz. tilapia
- 1 cup English cucumber, chopped with peel
- 2 T olive oil
- 1 sprig dill, chopped
- 1 Sweetener packet
- 3 T lime juice
- 2 T Cajun blackened seasoning

Directions

1. Mix the seasonings, except the Cajun blackened seasoning, into one bowl.
2. Add 1 T olive oil.
3. Emulsify or whip.
4. Pour the dressing over the cauliflower and cucumber.
5. Brush the fish with the olive oil on both sides.
6. Pour the other 1 T oil into a coated skillet.
7. Press the Cajun seasoning onto both sides of the fish.
8. Cook the fish in the olive oil 3 minutes per side.
9. Plate and serve.

Prep Instructions
Place all the veggies and dressing into one zip-lock bag.
Refrigerate.
Freeze each piece of fish individually in a zip-lock bag. Microwave
30 seconds to serve.

Chicken Parmesan over Protein Pasta

Prep time: 9 min; **Cook time:** 14 min
Serving Size: 2 oz. pasta, 1 cutlet; Serves: 4; **Calories:** 372
Total Fat: 18g; **Protein:** 56g; **Total Carbs:**7 g
Dietary Fiber: 2g; **Sugar:** 6g; **Sodium:** 1335mg

Ingredients

- 1 dash black pepper
- ½ tsp Italian spice mix
- 8 oz. Protein Plus Spaghetti
- ½ hand-shredded Parmesan
- 1 diced zucchini squash
- 1 ½ cups marinara sauce, any brand
- 24 oz. boneless thin chicken cutlets
- 2 T olive oil
- ½ cup grated Mozzarella cheese
- Water, for boiling the pasta

Directions

1. Boil the pasta with the zucchini in the water.
2. Mix the Italian spices and ¼ cup Parmesan cheese and place in a shallow dish.
3. Brush the chicken pieces with olive oil and press into spice and cheese to coat.
4. Place in skillet with the oil and cook until done.
5. Add the marinara sauce to the skillet to warm, cover the chicken if you desire.
6. Drain the pasta and zucchini, place on plates.
7. Top the chicken with the mozzarella and remaining Parmesan cheese.

8. Place sauce, chicken, and cheese onto spaghetti and serve.

Freezing Instructions
Make sure the spaghetti is covered with sauce, then freeze in containers. Microwave 3 minutes to serve.

Chicken Chow Mein Stir Fry

Prep time: 9 min; **Cook time:** 14 min;
Serving Size: 1/4; **Serves:** 4; **Calories:** 368
Total Fat: 18g; **Protein:** 42g; **Total Carbs:** 12g
Dietary Fiber: 16g; **Sugar:** 6g; **Sodium:** 746mg

Ingredients

- 1/2 cup sliced onion
- 2 T Oil, sesame garlic flavored
- 4 cups shredded Bok-Choy
- 1 c Sugar Snap Peas
- 1 cup fresh bean sprouts
- 3 stalks Celery, chopped
- 1 1/2 tsp minced Garlic
- 1 packet Splenda
- 1 cup Broth, chicken
- 2 T Soy Sauce
- 1 T ginger, freshly minced
- 1 tsp cornstarch
- 4 boneless Chicken Breasts, cooked/sliced thinly

Directions

1. Place the bok-choy, peas, celery in a skillet with 1 T garlic oil.
2. Stir fry until bok-choy is softened to liking.
3. Add remaining ingredients except the cornstarch.
4. If too thin, stir cornstarch into ½ cup cold water. When smooth pour into skillet.
5. Bring cornstarch and chow mein to a one-minute boil. Turn off the heat source.

6. Stir sauce then for wait 4 minutes to serve, after the chow mein has thickened.

Freezing Directions
Freeze in covered containers. Heat for 2 minutes in the microwave before serving

Colorful Chicken Casserole

Prep time: 14 min; **Cook time:** 14 min
Serving Size: 1 cup; **Serves:** 6; **Calories:** 412
Total Fat: 30g; **Protein:** 29; **Total Carbs:** 10g
Dietary Fiber: 9g; **Sugar:** 1g; **Sodium:** 712mg

Ingredients

- 1 cup broth, chicken
- 3 cups cooked chicken, diced
- 4 cups chopped broccoli
- 1 cup assorted colored bell peppers, chopped
- 1 cup cream
- 4 T sherry
- ¼ c hand-shredded Parmesan cheese
- 1 small size can black olives, sliced, drained
- 2 Tortilla Factory low-carb whole wheat tortillas
- ½ c hand-shredded mozzarella

Directions

1. Place broccoli and chicken broth into a skillet.
2. Top with lid, bring to a boil, and steam until desired crispness. (4 min)
3. Add the peppers, steam for one minute if you don't want them crisp.
4. Add the chicken and stir to heat.
5. Combine the sherry, cream, parmesan, and olives.
6. Tear the tortillas into bite-sized pieces.
7. Stir into the chicken and broccoli.
8. Pour cream sauce over the chicken, stir.
9. Top with hand-shredded mozzarella.
10. Broil in oven until cheese is melted and golden brown.

Freezing Directions
Place in covered containers to freeze. Microwave 2 minutes to serve.

Chicken Relleno Casserole

Prep time: 19 min; **Cook time:** 29 min
Serving Size: 1/6; **Serves:** 6; **Calories:** 265
Total Fat: 16g; **Protein:** 20g; **Total Carbs:** 18g
Dietary Fiber: 10g; **Sugar:** 0g; **Sodium:** 708mg

Ingredients

- 6 Tortilla Factory low-carb whole wheat tortillas, torn into small pieces
- 1 ½ cups hand-shredded cheese, Mexican
- 1 beaten egg
- 1 cup milk
- 2 cups cooked chicken, shredded
- 1 can Ro-tel
- ½ cup salsa verde

Directions

1. Grease an 8 x 8 glass baking dish
2. Heat oven to 375 degrees
3. Combine everything together, but reserve ½ cup of the cheese
4. Bake it for 29 minutes
5. Take it out of oven and add ½ cup cheese
6. Broil for about 2 minutes to melt the cheese

Freezing Instructions

Let the casserole cool. Slice into 6 pieces and place in freezer containers, (1 cup with lid)
Freeze. Microwave for 2 minutes to serve. Top with sour cream, if desired.

Italian Chicken with Asparagus and Artichoke Hearts

Prep time: 9 min; **Cook time:** 40 min
Serving Size: 1; **Serves:** 1; **Calories:** 435
Total Fat: 18g; **Protein:** 38g; **Total Carbs:** 16g
Dietary Fiber: 7g; **Sugar:** 1g; **Sodium:** 860mg

Ingredients

- 1 can long asparagus spears, drained
- 1 c red peppers, roasted, drained
- 1 c artichoke hearts, drained
- 6 oz. of boneless chicken breast, pounded thin or sliced thinly
- 2 T parmesan cheese
- 1 T Bisquick
- ½ tsp oregano
- ½ tsp garlic powder
- ½ cup fresh sliced mushrooms
- 2 T red wine vinegar
- 2 T butter
- 3 T olive oil

Directions

1. Place in a small blender container (or bowl) the oregano, garlic powder, vinegar, and 1 T oil. Place to the side.
2. Combine the Bisquick and Parmesan cheese.
3. Roll the chicken in the Bisquick and Parmesan mix.
4. Heat the butter in a skillet.
5. Brown the chicken on both sides and cook until done, approximately 4 minutes.
6. Emulsify or Quickly whip the wet ingredients you have placed to the side. This is your dressing.

7. Place the chicken on the plate.
8. Surround with the vegetables and drizzle them with the dressing.

Freezing Instructions
Freeze each serving of chicken in a zip-lock bag. Microwave for one minute before serving to break the chill, or two minutes to heat thoroughly. Place all the vegetables into one zip-lock bag with the dressing and refrigerate, or place the dressing separately in a cup.

Kabobs with Peanut Curry Sauce

Prep time: 9 min; **Cook time:** 9 min
Serving Size: 2 kabobs; **Serves:** 4; **Calories:** 530
Total Fat: 29g; **Protein:** 37g; **Total Carbs:** 6g
Dietary Fiber: 4g; **Sugar:** 2g; **Sodium:** 1538mg

Ingredients

- 1 cup Cream
- 4 tsp Curry Powder
- 1 1/2 tsp Cumin
- 1 1/2 tsp Salt
- 1 T minced garlic
- 1/3 cup Peanut Butter, sugar-free
- 2 T Lime Juice
- 3 T Water
- 1/2 small Onion, diced
- 2 T Soy Sauce
- 1 packet Splenda
- 8 oz. boneless, cooked Chicken Breast
- 8 oz. pork tenderloin

Directions

1. Blend together cream, onion, 2 tsp. garlic, curry and cumin powder, and salt.
2. Slice the meats into 1 inch pieces.
3. Place the cream sauce into a bowl and put in the chicken and tenderloin to marinate. Let rest in sauce for 14 minutes.
4. Blend peanut butter, water, 1 tsp. garlic, lime juice, soy sauce, and Splenda. This is your peanut dipping sauce.

5. Remove the meats and thread on skewers. Broil or grill 4 minutes per side until meat is done.
6. Serve with dipping sauce.

Prep Directions
Place the meat into zip-lock bags and freeze. Place the peanut sauce and the cream sauce in the fridge in covered containers.

Pizza

Prep time: 4 min; **Cook time:** 4 min
Serving Size: 1; **Serves:** 1; **Calories:** 155
Total Fat: 7g; **Protein:** 13g; **Total Carbs:** 18g
Dietary Fiber: 10g; **Sugar:** 2g; **Sodium:** 741mg

Ingredients

- 1 Tortilla Factory low carb whole wheat tortilla
- ¼ cup mozzarella cheese, hand-shredded
- ¼ cup tomato paste
- sprinkle of Italian seasoning
- sprinkle of garlic salt
- Cut the broccoli, spinach, mushrooms, peppers, and onions you like for toppings

Directions

1. Turn broiler on in oven, or toaster oven
2. Spread tortilla with tomato paste
3. Sprinkle seasoning on the paste
4. Add the cheese
5. Add the veggies
6. Broil or toast 1-4 minutes until crust is crunchy and cheese melted

Freezing Instructions

Place when cooled into individual freezer bags. Microwave for 1 minute to refresh.

Salmon with Bok-Choy

Prep time: 9 min; **Cook time:** 9 min;
Serving Size: 1; **Serves:** 4; **Calories:** 410
Total Fat: 30g; **Protein:** 30g; **Total Carbs:** 7g
Dietary Fiber: 2g; **Sugar:** 0g; **Sodium:** 200mg

Ingredients

- 1 c red peppers, roasted, drained
- 2 cups chopped bok-choy
- 1 T salted butter
- 5 oz. salmon steak
- 1 lemon, sliced very thinly
- ⅛ tsp black pepper
- 1 T olive oil
- 2 T sriracha sauce

Directions

1. Place oil in skillet
2. Place all but 4 slices of lemon in the skillet.
3. Sprinkle the bok choy with the black pepper.
4. Stir fry the bok-choy with the lemons.
5. Remove and place on four plates.
6. Place the butter in the skillet and stir fry the salmon, turning once.
7. Place the salmon on the bed of bok-choy.
8. Divide the red peppers and encircle the salmon.
9. Place a slice of lemon atop the salmon.
10. Drizzle with sriracha sauce.

Freezing Instructions

Freeze the cooked salmon in individual zip-lock bags. Place the bok-choy, with the remaining ingredients into one cup containers. Microwave the salmon for one minute and the frozen bok choy for two. Assemble to serve.

Sriracha Tuna Kabobs

Prep time: 4 min; **Cook time:** 9 min;
Serving Size: 2 kabobs; **Serves:** 4; **Calories:** 467
Total Fat: 18g; **Protein:** 56g; **Total Carbs:** 21g
Dietary Fiber: 3.5g; **Sugar:** 6g; **Sodium:** 433mg

Ingredients

- 4 T Huy Fong chili garlic sauce
- 1 T sesame oil infused with garlic
- 1 T ginger, fresh, grated
- 1 T garlic, minced
- 1 red onion, cut into quarters and separated by petals
- 2 cups bell peppers, red, green, yellow
- 1 can whole water chestnuts, cut in half
- ½ pound fresh mushrooms, halved
- 32 oz. boneless tuna, chunks or steaks
- 1 Splenda packet
- 2 zucchini, sliced 1 inch thick, keep skins on

Directions

1. Layer the tuna and the vegetable pieces evenly onto 8 skewers.
2. Combine the spices and the oil and chili sauce, add the Splenda
3. Quickly blend, either in blender or by Quickly whipping.
4. Brush onto the kabob pieces, make sure every piece is coated
5. Grill 4 minutes on each side, check to ensure the tuna is cooked to taste.
6. Serving size is two skewers.

Prep Directions
Mix the marinade ingredients and store in covered container in the fridge. Place all the vegetables in one container in the fridge. Place the tuna in a separate zip-lock bag.

Steak Salad with Asian Spice

Prep time: 4 min; **Cook time:** 4 min
Serving Size: 1/2; **Serves:** 2; **Calories:** 350
Total Fat: 23g; **Protein:** 28g; **Total Carbs:** 7g
Dietary Fiber: 3.5; **Sugar:** 0; **Sodium:** 267mg

Ingredients

- 2 T sriracha sauce
- 1 T garlic, minced
- 1 T ginger, fresh, grated
- 1 bell pepper, yellow, cut in thin strips
- 1 bell pepper, red, cut in thin strips
- 1 T sesame oil, garlic
- 1 Splenda packet
- ½ tsp curry powder
- ½ tsp rice wine vinegar
- 8 oz. of beef sirloin, cut into strips
- 2 cups baby spinach, stemmed
- ½ head butter lettuce, torn or chopped into bite-sized pieces

Directions

1. Place the garlic, sriracha sauce, 1 tsp sesame oil, rice wine vinegar, and Splenda into a bowl and combine well.
2. Pour half of this mix into a zip-lock bag. Add the steak to marinade while you are preparing the salad.
3. Assemble the brightly colored salad by layering in two bowls.
4. Place the baby spinach into the bottom of the bowl.
5. Place the butter lettuce next.
6. Mix the two peppers and place on top.

7. Remove the steak from the marinade and discard the liquid and bag.
8. Heat the sesame oil and quickly stir fry the steak until desired doneness, it should take about 3 minutes.
9. Place the steak on top of the salad.
10. Drizzle with the remaining dressing (other half of marinade mix).
11. Sprinkle sriracha sauce across the salad.

Prep Instructions

Combine the salad ingredients and place in zip-lock bag in the fridge. Mix the marinade and halve into 2 zip-lock bags. Place the sriracha sauce into a small sealed container. Slice the steak and freeze in a zip-lock bag with the marinade. To prepare, mix the ingredients like the initial directions. Stir fry the marinated beef for 4 minutes to take into consideration the beef is frozen.

Tilapia and Broccoli

Prep time: 4 min; **Cook time:** 14 min;
Serving Size: 1; **Serves:** 1; **Calories:** 362
Total Fat: 25g; **Protein:** 29g; **Total Carbs:** 3.5g
Dietary Fiber: 3g; **Sugar:** 0g; **Sodium:** 0mg

Ingredients

- 6 oz. tilapia, frozen is fine
- 1 T butter
- 1 T garlic, minced or finely chopped
- 1 tsp of lemon pepper seasoning
- 1 cup broccoli florets, fresh or frozen, but fresh will be crisper

Directions

1. Set the pre-warmed oven for 350 degrees.
2. Place the fish in an aluminum foil packet.
3. Arrange the broccoli around the fish to make an attractive arrangement.
4. Sprinkle the lemon pepper on the fish.
5. Close the packet and seal, bake for 14 minutes.
6. Combine the garlic and butter. Set aside.
7. Remove the packet from the oven and transfer ingredients to a plate.
8. Place the butter on the fish and broccoli.

Prep Instructions

Place the butter and garlic into small sealed containers or zip-lock bags, Refrigerate or freeze. Cut the broccoli (if fresh) and place in zip-lock bags in the fridge. Place the lemon pepper into a small container.

Chapter 5: Super-Food Snacks

Berry -Choco-Cherry Protein Bars

Prep time: 4 min; **Cook time:** 10 min
Serving Size: 1 bar; **Serves:** 12; **Calories:** 235
Total Fat: 17g; **Protein:** 8g; **Total Carbs:** 6g
Dietary Fiber: 4g; **Sugar:** 11g; **Sodium:** 141mg

Ingredients

- ½ c sliced almonds
- 1 c chocolate Protein Powder
- ½ c pecan pieces
- ½ c fresh cherries, pitted
- ¼ c fresh blueberries
- ¼ c unsweetened shredded coconut
- ½ c almond butter
- ¼ c coconut oil
- ¼ c almond meal
- 1 tsp vanilla
- 2 eggs
- ½ tsp salt
- ½ c low-carb baking mix
- 2 packets Splenda

Directions

1. Butter a glass loaf pan.
2. Set the oven to 325 F.
3. Mix all of the ingredients except the fruit.
4. Carefully fold the berries and cherries into the batter.
5. Pour into the prepared pan.

6. Bake for 10 minutes.
7. Let cool 10 minutes.
8. Cut into 12 bars.

Freezing Instructions
Place into individual servings in snack-sized zip-lock bags.

Brie Stuffed with Smoked Salmon

Prep time: 4 min; **Cook time:** 0 min
Serving Size: 1/4; **Serves:** 4; **Calories:** 241
Total Fat: 19g; **Protein:** 18g; **Total Carbs:** 0g
Dietary Fiber: 0g; **Sugar:** 0g; **Sodium:** 668mg

Ingredients

- 8 oz. Brie round
- 1 T fresh dill
- 2 T lemon juice
- Smoked Salmon, 4 oz.

Directions

1. Slice round of Brie in half lengthwise.
2. Spread the surface with the salmon, then the dill, then sprinkle with the lemon juice.
3. Place top of Brie back onto the bottom.

Serve with

- Jicama
- Celery sticks
- Cauliflower bites

Buffalo Chicken Dip

Prep time: 19 min; **Cook time:** 9 min;
Serving Size: 8 sticks; **Serves:** 4; **Calories:** 286
Total Fat: 20g; **Protein:** 19g; **Total Carbs:** 2g
Dietary Fiber: 2g; **Sugar:** 0g; **Sodium:** 471mg

Ingredients

- 6 eggs
- water
- 6 oz. cooked chicken
- 3 T mayonnaise
- 1 ½ T red hot buffalo wing sauce with no sugar
- ¼ c blue cheese, crumbled
- 8 celery stalks

Directions

1. Boil the eggs for 9 min. Cool and dice.
2. Chop the chicken finely.
3. Slice the celery into 2-inch long pieces.
4. Mix all ingredients excluding the celery in a bowl.
5. Fill the celery sticks and divide into four servings.
6. Dip into individual ramekins of hot sauce for more zing.

Prep Instructions

Combine the filling, separate into 4 closed containers. Refrigerate.
Cut the celery and place in zip-lock bags. Refrigerate.

Chinese Fried Dumplings

Prep time: 19 min; **Cook time:** 9 min
Serving Size: 4 dumplings; **Serves:** 4; **Calories:** 278
Total Fat: 13g; **Protein:** 20g; **Total Carbs:** 22g
Dietary Fiber: 6g; **Sugar:** 3g; **Sodium:** 975mg

Ingredients

- 1 T- Vegetable Oil
- 2 T Soy Sauce, Low Salt
- 2 T Chopped Parsley
- 1 Egg, beaten
- 1/8 tsp, Black Pepper
- 1 1/2 T Ginger root - Raw
- 4 T Garlic
- 14 oz. Tofu
- 1/8 tsp Salt
- 1/2 c Baby Bok Choy, chopped finely
- ½ c Onions chopped very fine
- 4 Green Onions, chop the green tops finely and set aside. Save the white parts.
- 16 4-inch Dumpling Wrappers

Directions

1. In a skillet, cook the garlic, ginger and chopped onions together in the vegetable until the onion is translucent.
2. Add the tofu and parsley and cook until the tofu is golden-colored.
3. Add the soy sauce and cook until the filling in the skillet is dry. Stir in the salt, pepper, parsley, pepper, salt, finely chopped bok-choy, and the tops of the green onions.
4. Remove from the skillet and stir in the egg thoroughly.

5. Drain in a fine screened colander, pressing the mixture firmly into the colander to remove all the fluid.
6. Slice the white parts of the green onions very thinly.
7. Take the dumpling wrapper and place in your hand. Take one heaping tablespoon of the filling and place it in the middle of the wrapper. Dip your finger in cold water, running it on the inside edge of the wrapper. Press to seal.
8. Take the 16 dumplings and place in a skillet to fry in oil.
9. Brown the dumplings, then place a lid on the skillet for 5 minutes.
10. Turn the dumplings and let steam in the skillet another 5 minutes.
11. Place on a plate with a small ramekin of soy sauce. Sprinkle the soy sauce with the white pieces of the green onion.

Prep Instructions

Prepare the filling and refrigerate. Prepare the dipping sauce and refrigerate. Assembly the dumplings and fry.

Chipotle Kale Chips

Prep time: 4 min; **Cook time:** 29 min
Serving Size: 1/6; **Serves:** 6; **Calories:** 37
Total Fat: 3g; **Protein:** 1g; **Total Carbs:** 2.7g
Dietary Fiber: 1g; **Sugar:** 0g; **Sodium:** 95mg

Ingredients

- 2 large bunches kale, chopped into 4 inch pieces and stemmed
- 1 T Olive oil
- ⅛ tsp salt
- 1 tsp chipotle powder
- ¼ cup very finely hand-shredded parmesan cheese

Directions

1. Wash and dry the kale, cutting into 4 inch pieces
2. Set oven at 250 F.
3. Line 3 baking sheets
4. Put the kale in a bowl, then hand coat with the olive oil, chipotle, and parmesan cheese
5. Place on the baking sheet with no pieces touching
6. Bake for 19 minutes and then check for dryness and crispiness
7. Bake another 9 minutes if necessary.

Storage Instructions
Can be stored for one week in an airtight container.

Crunchy Hot Chicken Kabobs

Prep time: 12 min; **Cook time:** 21 min
Serving Size: 1 skewer; **Serves:** 4; **Calories:** 363
Total Fat: 20g; **Protein:** 37g; **Total Carbs:** 8g
Dietary Fiber: 2g; **Sugar:** 4g; **Sodium:** 170mg

Ingredients

- ½ c lemon juice
- 1/4 cup extra virgin olive oil
- 3 T garlic, minced
- 1 teaspoon artificial sweetener
- 1/2 teaspoon dried crushed red pepper
- 1 teaspoon ground cumin
- 1 teaspoon chili powder
- 2 pounds (about 8 small) boneless chicken thighs
- 8 radishes, thinly sliced
- 16 Grape tomatoes
- 8 cherries, halved and pitted
- 2 jalapenos, fresh, sliced into 4 pieces
- 1 cup jicama, cut into 8 pieces

Directions

1. Combine the lemon juice, olive oil, garlic, crushed red pepper, cumin and chili powder into a marinade/sauce. Separate into two servings.
2. Place the chicken into an oven safe pan and cover with one half of the sauce. Broil for ten minutes, then remove the chicken and turn. Broil for another ten minutes.
3. Cut the chicken into 4 pieces each. Thread on a kabob skewer as follows, grape tomato, ½ radish, ½ cherry, 1

piece of jalapeno, 1 piece jicama, chicken piece. Continue alternating until skewer is full.

4. Make 4 skewers. Take the remaining marinade sauce and brush the kabobs thoroughly, using all of the sauce.
5. Place under the broiler for 1 minute to roast the grapes and cherries.

Prepping Instructions

Combine the marinade sauce and keep it in a covered cup in the fridge. Cut the vegetables and place in the fridge in a zip-lock bag. Keep the chicken in the fridge until time to cook. Leftovers can be removed from the skewer, stored in the refrigerator in a zip-lock bag, and placed onto a salad of spinach, romaine and kale for a lunch treat.

Edamame Dip

Prep time: 5 min; **Cook time:** 5 min
Serving Size: 1/2c; **Serves:** 5; **Calories:** 104
Total Fat: 3g; **Protein:** 9g; **Total Carbs:** 8g
Dietary Fiber: 3g; **Sugar:** 3g; **Sodium:** 136mg

Ingredients

- 2 cups edamame, peas only
- ½ c plain Greek yogurt
- 1 tsp cumin
- 2 tsp sriracha sauce
- 1 tsp soy sauce
- 1 T minced garlic
- 2 T lime juice

Directions

1. Combine all ingredients into the blender jar and emulsify. Serve with zucchini fries.

Prepping Instructions

Mix in a blender and store in a covered container placed in the fridge. Will stay fresh for three days.

Granola

Prep time: 16 min; **Cook time:** 0 min
Serving Size: 1/3c; **Serves:** 1; **Calories:** 449
Total Fat: 34g; **Protein:** 25.3g; **Total Carbs:** 2.4g
Dietary Fiber: 6.8g; **Sugar:** 0g; **Sodium:** 479mg

Ingredients

- 1 oz. cocoa flavored Sacha Inchi Seeds
- 1 oz. gruyere cheese, finely chopped
- 1 oz. pepitas, roasted

Directions

1. Combine all ingredients in a zip-lock bag and give it a little shake, to mix evenly. One bag equals one serving.

Storage Instructions
Can be stored in an airtight container for one week.

Jalapeno Poppers

Prep time: 6 min; **Cook time:** 15 min
Serving Size: 2; **Serves:** 9; **Calories:** 139
Total Fat: 11g; **Protein:** 7g; **Total Carbs:** 1g
Dietary Fiber: 1g; **Sugar:** 1g; **Sodium:** 236mg

Ingredients

- 9 Peppers, jalapeno, raw, cut in half lengthwise
- 4 oz. Cheese, cream
- 1/4 cup, Salsa Verde
- 0.50 cup finely diced cauliflower
- 4 oz. Pepper Jack Cheese, hand-grated finely
- 9 slices, Thin Cut Bacon, cut in half

Directions

1. Set the oven at 375 F. Slice the jalapenos and remove the seeds. Set to the side.
2. Mix the cheese, salsa, and cauliflower for the filling. Set to the side to mellow.
3. Place the bacon on a paper towel and microwave for 30 seconds. You want it to be soft but not done.
4. Fill the peppers with the cheese mixture and then wrap with the bacon. Secure the bacon with a toothpick.
5. Place in the oven for 15 minutes.
6. Turn on the oven to broil. Place under the broiler for 2 minutes so the bacon will be crunchy.

Prepping Instructions

Combine the cheese mixture and place in the fridge. Placing the jalapenos on top of the cheese mixture in the refrigerated container will give the cheese a hotter taste.

Mushroom Frittata

Prep time: 9 min; **Cook time:** 44 min
Serving Size: 1/6; **Serves:** 6; **Calories:** 297
Total Fat: 2g; **Protein:** 25g; **Total Carbs:** 4g
Dietary Fiber: 2g; **Sugar:** 2g; **Sodium:** 287mg

Ingredients

- 2 T butter
- 12 Eggs
- 4 oz. baby spinach, diced
- 3/4 cup fontina cheese, diced
- ½ cup chopped red onion
- 1 cup sliced Mushrooms
- ½ cup Greek yogurt, plain
- 1/8 tsp of nutmeg

Directions

1. Set oven to 350F.
2. Using an iron skillet, heat 1 T of butter in the skillet
3. Add onions and mushroom, cook until onions are glassy and water is gone.
4. Quickly whip eggs, sour cream, and spinach in a bowl. Add in ½ cup cheese.
5. Add the butter to the skillet with the onions and mushrooms.
6. Set the burner to medium and pour in the egg mixture. Do not stir.
7. Cook about 4 minutes, until eggs look set.
8. Remove from burner, sprinkle with the remaining cheese.
9. Transfer to the oven.

10. Bake 29 minutes. Center should be set.

Freezing Instructions
Place cooled frittata in zip-lock bags and freeze.

Salsa Chicken Bites

Prep time: 4 min; **Cook time:** 14 min
Serving Size: 1; **Serves:** 2; **Calories:** 359
Total Fat: 14g; **Protein:** 43g; **Total Carbs:** 14g
Dietary Fiber: 2g; **Sugar:** 9g; **Sodium:** 1306mg

Ingredients

- 2 Chicken Breasts
- 1 cup Salsa, red or green
- 1 Taco Seasoning Mix
- 1 cup plain Greek Yogurt
- ½ cup cheddar Cheese cubes

Directions

1. In a skillet, place the chicken breasts, ½ cup of salsa, and taco seasoning mix.
2. Cook on medium until chicken is done, about 12-14 minutes.
3. Take the chicken out, and cube.
4. Place on toothpicks, topping with the cheddar cheese cubes.
5. Place yogurt and remaining salsa in cups for dipping.

Freezing Instructions

Freeze the chicken in individual serving portions in closed containers. Place the yogurt and salsa in the fridge.

Smoked Salmon Dip

Prep time: 6 min; **Cook time:** 0 min
Serving Size: all; **Serves**: 1; **Calories:** 229
Total Fat: 14g; **Protein:** 19g; **Total Carbs:** 6g
Dietary Fiber: 4g; **Sugar:** 9g; **Sodium:** 572mg

Ingredients

- 3 oz. smoked salmon
- 1 can tomatoes and jalapenos
- 2 T cream cheese
- 1 cup sliced celery sticks

Directions

1. Combine everything but the celery in the blender or food processor to emulsify.
2. Spread onto celery sticks.

Prep Instructions

Place dip in a closed container. Place celery sticks in a zip-lock bag or place in water in a closed container. Refrigerate.

Spinach Dip

Prep time: 4 min; **Cook time:** 0 min
Serving Size: 1/4; **Serves:** 4; **Calories:** 101
Total Fat: 4g; **Protein:** 10g; **Total Carbs:** 5g
Dietary Fiber: 5g; **Sugar:** 4g; **Sodium:** 183mg

Ingredients

- 10 oz., Spinach, Raw
- 1 ½ c Greek Yogurt
- 1 T onion powder
- 1/2 tsp garlic salt
- black pepper to taste
- ½ tsp Greek Seasoning

Directions

1. Place all ingredients in blender.
2. Emulsify. Taste. Adjust seasonings.
3. Serve.

Storage Instructions
Place in portion-sized containers in the fridge.

Vietnamese Spring Rolls with Peanut Sauce

Prep time: 15 min; **Cook time:** 10 min
Serving Size: 1 cup; **Serves:** 3; **Calories:** 231
Total Fat: 10g; **Protein:** 22g; **Total Carbs:** 12g
Dietary Fiber: 3g; **Sugar:** 3g; **Sodium:** 456mg

Ingredients

- 6 Boston or Bibb lettuce leaves
- ½ cup parsley, fresh, coarsely chopped
- ½ cup purple cabbage, coarsely chopped
- 1 T salsa verde
- 2 tsp soy sauce
- 1 T garlic infused olive oil
- 20 snow peas, fresh
- 1 T ginger, grated fresh
- 1 T garlic, minced fresh
- 1 packet artificial sweetener
- 2 T sugar-free peanut butter
- ½ cup radishes, thinly sliced
- ½ cup cooked wild rice
- 1 yellow pepper, diced
- 1 T tabasco sauce, hot
- 2 T lime juice
- 8 oz. boneless pork chops

Directions

1. Combine the salsa verde, ginger, garlic, artificial sweetener, peanut butter, tabasco sauce and lime juice in a blender and emulsify. This is your peanut sauce.

2. Place the wild rice, yellow pepper, radishes, purple cabbage, and parsley into a bowl and mix together.
3. Cut the pork chops into even pieces, about one inch sized. Stir fry them quickly in a wok or hot skillet, adding the garlic oil and soy sauce while cooking.
4. Lay the six lettuce leaves flat on the table.
5. Spoon the cabbage mixture into the leaves, ½ cup per leaf.
6. Place the pork chop pieces on top, divided between the 6 leaves.
7. Drizzle the peanut sauce onto each spring roll.
8. Roll the leaves and fold like a burrito to serve.

Prepping Instructions

Combine the filling ingredients in a bowl and place in the fridge. Pre-cook the pork chops and soy sauce and oil, place in the fridge in a covered container. Prepare the peanut sauce and refrigerate. Microwave the meat before filling the spring rolls.

Zucchini and Asparagus Fries

Prep time: 9 min; **Cook time:** 20 min
Serving Size: 20 fries; **Serves:** 2; **Calories:** 372
Total Fat: 24g; **Protein:** 24g; **Total Carbs:** 11g
Dietary Fiber: 7g; **Sugar:** 6g; **Sodium:** 484mg

Ingredients

- 1 egg
- ¼ c Low Carb Baking Mix
- 2 T Olive oil
- ½ finely chopped jalapeno pepper
- 20 fresh asparagus spears, lightly steamed
- 2 Zucchini squash
- ½ c Parmesan, finely hand-grated
- 1/8 tsp freshly ground black pepper

Directions

1. Set the oven at 400 F.
2. Prepare a shallow baking pan, 9 x 13 or larger, by lining it with parchment paper or foil.
3. Cut the zucchini squash into sixths, lengthwise, and then cut in half to make a "French fry" shape.
4. Place 2 flat bottomed dishes on the table for dipping the squash and asparagus. (a pie tin is good)
5. Place the low-carb baking mix, the chopped jalapeno pepper, and the parmesan cheese into one dish.
6. Beat the egg until frothy in the second dish.
7. Carefully dip the squash and asparagus into first the egg, then roll in the cheese mixture.
8. Place each squash or asparagus fry onto the lined baking pan, separating them so the sides aren't touching.

9. Drizzle the tops with the olive oil. Then sprinkle tops with the black pepper.
10. Bake at 400 F for 10 minutes, remove them from the oven and turn, then bake for approximately another 10 minutes.
11. Place under the broiler for one minute for crispiness.

Freezing Instructions
Place each serving in a zip-lock bag to freeze. Heat in the oven at 400 F for ten minutes to refresh.

Printed in Great Britain
by Amazon